Main St Mgr

JLK

Armenian

Main St.

American Retro

SOURCEBOOKS, INC.
NAPERVILLE, ILLINOIS

Main St.

American Retro

All streets are theaters.

Ronald Blythe

Contents

Introduction

"On that road the nation is steadily traveling beyond the troubles of this century, constantly heading toward finer tomorrows. The American Road is paved with hope."

1951 Ford ad

The great highways of America were its very heart and soul. They spanned the limits of this vast country from top to bottom and east to west. They carried the new breed of motorists from good to bad, from boom to bust, through towns with such names as Mammoth Cave, Kentucky; Pleasantville, New York; and Broken Bow, Nebraska; many of them with nothing more than a Main Street and a drugstore.

Along the way these arteries offered succor in the form of welcoming diners, serving plates of wholesome freshly prepared dishes—food that spawned a universal language in the shape of hot dogs, hamburgers, fries, and malts. Comfortable motels with warm rooms offered the latest in modern conveniences, from power showers to the combination television and radio set, and provided a safe haven for the night. They were clean and affordable family businesses, which allowed the nuclear family, for the first time, to explore the wonders of their own land.

Parked outside were the trappings of prosperity—Cadillacs, T-Birds, Chevrolets, and Corvettes—cars that any sane person has always wanted to drive. These were elongated giants, explosions of chrome grilles and wire wheels, creating fantasies of speed and escapism with features taken from aircraft designs and space travel. These were the only beasts capable of taming this extraordinary country, and are as representative of the United States of America as the Statue of Liberty or the Stars and Stripes.

The names of those great roads—Highway 61, Route 66, Pacific 1—have since passed into popular mythology. For those with a passion for adventure the names evoke images of *Easy Rider*, and the lyrics of Bob Dylan and the Rolling Stones. At the same time, they are able to convey that air of safety and innocence, when mom and pop ushered the kids into the back of the family automobile and headed off on vacation.

Now this golden age is all but gone, although remnants do remain. The highways have fallen into disrepair, superseded by freeways with no recognizable character. Many diners have served their last "special," and a large number of "ma and pa" motels have been swallowed up into chains with such alluring names as Comfort Inn and Motel 6 (we are never told what happened to Motels 1 through 5). Small towns, with the whole of life encapsulated on Main Street, are a far cry from the soulless shopping malls of today. And the cars—oh those glorious, gas-guzzling monsters—have been replaced by sensible, compact, economical models with dull names.

As a tribute to the post-war period when people had money in their pockets and a hankering to spend it, the four titles in the *American Retro* series draw on images, both retro and modern, that resonate with the spirit of '50s America. These pictures are paired with advertising slogans, popular sayings, puns, and quotations from personalities that fully illustrate an age when being economical with the truth came naturally to the advertisers and salesmen of the day, who were desperate to paint a dazzling and futuristic world in which everyone could share. Motels shamelessly claimed to offer comfort fit for the "Queen of Sheba"; car manufacturers used such buzz words as "Rocket Ride" and "Glamorous new Futuramics"; and diners bedecked themselves in chrome detailing and neon lights.

The *American Retro* series recaptures a little of what made those times so special, with images that will fill those that lived through that age with nostalgia and gently amuse and inform those who did not. Read, remember, and enjoy.

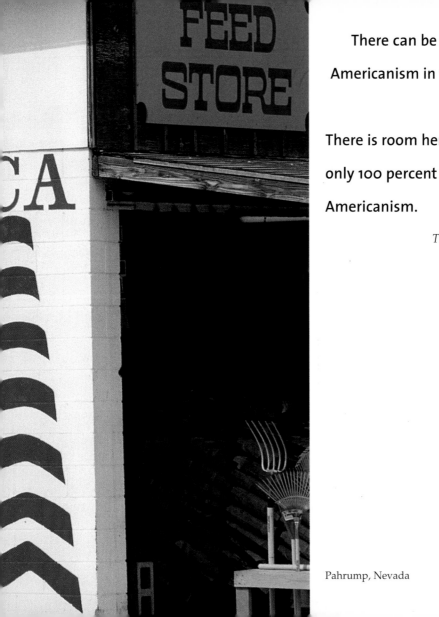

There can be no fifty-fifty Americanism in this country.

There is room here for only 100 percent Americanism.

Theodore Roosevelt

There's a bank in California that has a "western window" for those who are quick on the draw.

Bodie ghost town, California

Too bad that

all the people

who know how

to run the country

are busy driving taxicabs

and cutting hair.

George Burns

Hollywood, California

A small town newspaper advertised, "Read your Bible to know what people ought to do. Read this paper to know what they actually do."

San Francisco, California

I like the silent church

before the service begins,

better than any preaching.

Ralph Waldo Emerson

In a hick town they give you credit for resisting temptation—

and a lot more credit for finding any.

Groveland, California

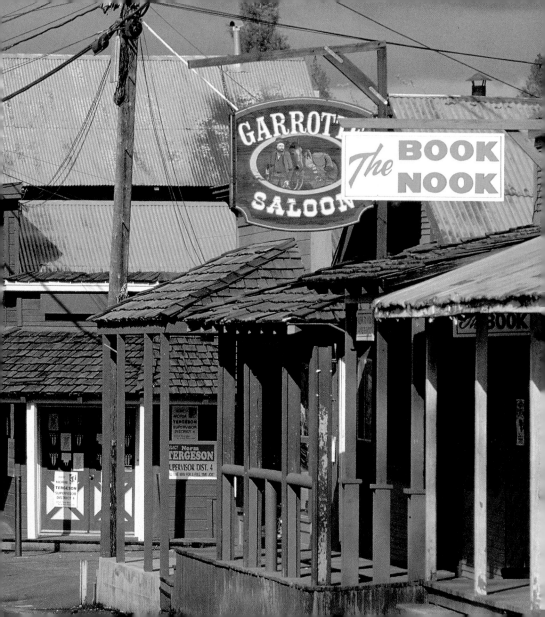

Sit a spell...

The grass is always greener

on the other side of town.

Main Street in a Wyoming town

They say the cows laid out Boston.

Well, there are worse surveyors.

Ralph Waldo Emerson

Boston Common, Massachusetts

Man cannot live on bread alone. Sometimes he needs a Danish.

You can tell a lot about a fellow's

character by his way of eating jelly beans.

Ronald Reagan

Hain't we got all the fools in
town on our side?

And hain't that a big enough
majority in any town?

Mark Twain

Skagway, Alaska

WOODSTO[CK]

VINS–Vermont Institute of Na[tural]
   Woodstock Historical Soci[ety]
     Billings Farm and Muse[um]

Saturdays M.T. Tom Farmers[Market]
Thro Oct VINS Wildlife Ant Exhi[bit]
Fri 27 Bloodmobile 12:30–5:30 [P.M.]
Fri 29 Pumkin Carving evening
Sat 28 Knitting Workshop–Dag[..]
Sat 28–Tues 31 End of Season Sale
Thus 26 Fri 27 Sat 28 Sleepy Hallow–Yoh[..]
Mon 30 Religion and Politics disc[ussion]
Mon 30 Harvest Social Mixer 5:30
Sat 28 Junk Mail + Magazine[..]

Sun 29 A Family Halloween– noon [..]
Fri 27 + Sat 28 Haunted House + Hay R[ide]
Fri 29 Pumkin Carving + Displa[y]
Fri 27 Halloween Dance Benefit [..]

Free Firewood for Seniors deliv[ered]

Many a small thing
has been made large
by the right kind
of advertising.

Mark Twain

We grew up founding our dreams

on the infinite promise

of American advertising.

Zelda Fitzgerald

When Hungry. Thirsty

DRIN

Dr.Pepp

GOOD FOR LIFE

at

O'clock

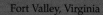

Fort Valley, Virginia

No city should be too large
for a man to walk out of it
in a morning.

Cyril Connolly

There are three kinds of people; those that make things happen, those that watch things happen, and those who don't know what's happening.

The difference between

antique and junk

depends on

who's selling what to whom.

Selma, Alabama

The mail must get through

come hell or high water.

Chicago, Illinois

Smoking is one of the leading causes of statistics.

Fletcher Knebel

Cigar Store, Butte, Montana

Once it was ambition that kept people on the move.

Now it's "No Parking" signs.

All streets are theaters.

Ronald Blythe

For a place with a bad location

and no neon sign,

we're doing a heck of a business.

Rosalind Russell

　　　　　　　Palmyra, Wisconsin

It's not so much a one horse town.

They are still saving up to buy the horse.

A city that sleeps,

and sleeps...

I can't say I was ever lost,

but I was bewildered
once for three days.

Daniel Boone

The ghost town of
Bannack, Montana

Trapped in the One Way

system...

San Francisco, California

I used to work in a fire hydrant factory.

You couldn't park anywhere near the place.

Steven Wright

Extravagance is anything you buy that you can't put on a credit card.

Eagles Mere, Pennsylvania

Superior, Nebraska

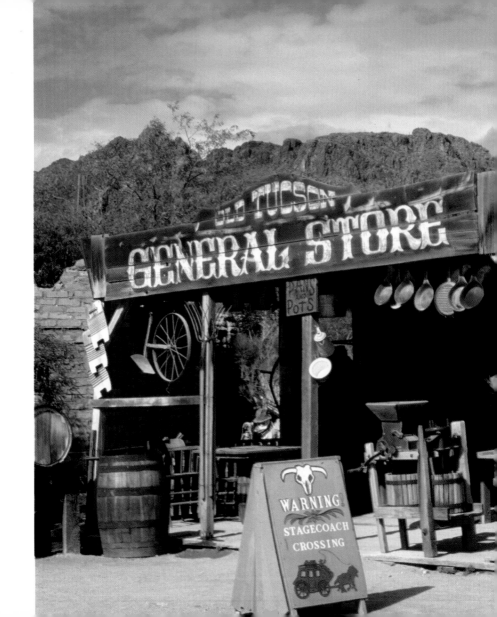

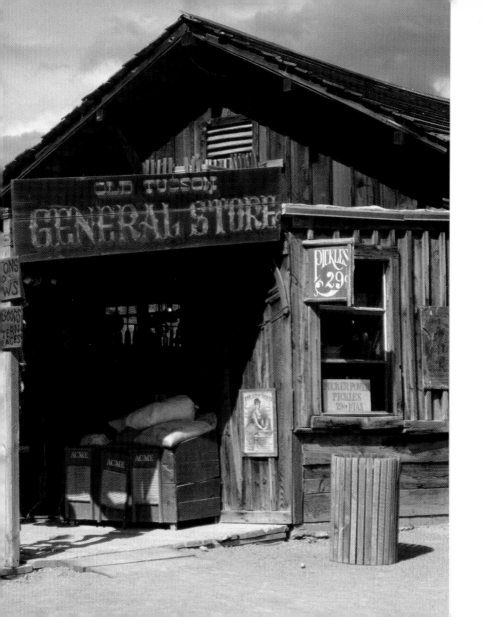

Always do right;

this will gratify some people

and astonish the rest.

Mark Twain

Manchester, Vermont

Ever notice how road signs can be so bossy?

Advice to motorists:

If you want to stay in the pink, watch the red and green.

Woodinville, Washington

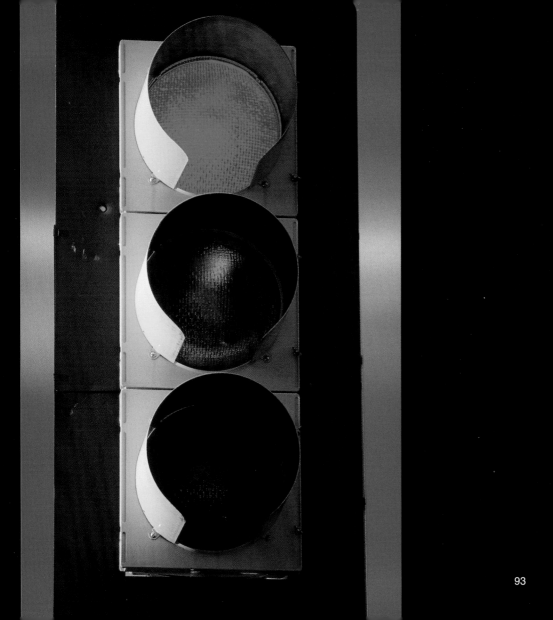

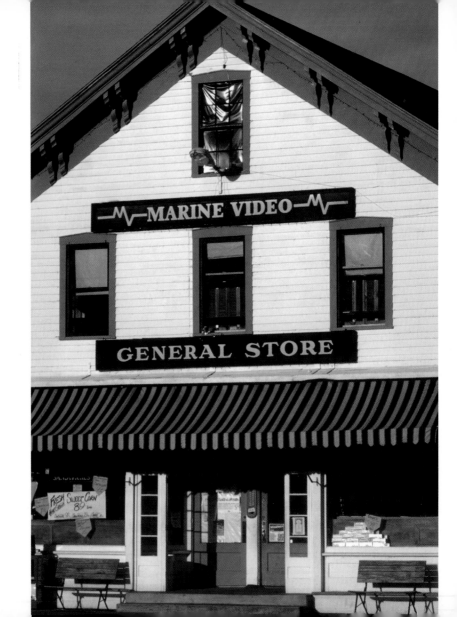

There is no point at which you can say,

"Well, I'm successful now. I might as well take a nap."

Carrie Fisher

Good salesmen, like good cooks, create an appetite when the buyer doesn't seem to be hungry.

Reality is merely an illusion,

albeit a very persistent one.

Albert Einstein

Nevada City ghost town, Montana

Hurricane,
Utah

MINE SHAFT

Why don't you come up

and see me sometime?

Picture credits

All images reproduced by permission of Corbis Images unless otherwise stated.

Page 8/9: Corner of Main and Maple Street, Lyndonville, Vermont; credit Joseph Sohm.

Page 10/11: American flag painted on the side of Western store in Pahrump, Nevada; reproduced by permission of Travel Ink/Walter Wolfe.

Page 12/13: Main Street storefronts in Litangston, Montana; credit Kevin R. Morris.

Page 14/15: Ghost town in Bodie State Historic Park, California; credit Robert Holmes.

Page 16/17: Barber shop façade in Hollywood, California; credit The Purcell Team.

Page 18/19: Pub sign in Bar Harbor, Maine; credit Roman Soumar.

Page 20/21: Newspaper vending machines in San Francisco, California; credit Robert Holmes.

Page 22/23: Methodist church in Bay City, Oregon; reproduced by permission of Travel Ink/Ken Gibson.

Page 24/25: Main Street of Groveland, California; credit Nik Wheeler.

Page 26/27: Town store in Redwoods, California; credit Nik Wheeler.

Page 28/29: Rabbit Hash General Store, Kentucky; credit Philip Gould.

Page 30/31: Main Street in a Wyoming town; credit Kevin R. Morris.

Page 32/33: Boston, Massachusetts; reproduced by permission of Travel Ink/Ken Gibson.

Page 34/35: Bakery in New York City; credit Raymon Gehman.

Page 36/37: "Don't Walk" sign in New York City; credit Owen Franken.

Page 38/39: Candy machines in New York City; credit Roger Wood.

Page 40/41: Old West town; credit Craig Aurness.

Page 42/43: Red Onion Saloon in Skagway, Alaska; credit Wolfgang Kaehler.

Page 44/45: Kiosk in Woodstock, Vermont; credit Phil Schermeister.

Page 46/47: Dr. Gravity's Kite Shop in Harwich, Massachusetts; credit James Marshall.

Page 48/49: St. David's Grocery in Fort Valley, Virginia; credit William A. Bake.

Page 50/51: Grand Teton National Park, Wyoming; reproduced by permission of Travel Ink/Ken Gibson.

Page 52/53: Silverton, Colorado; credit Craig Aurness.

Page 54/55: Feed Store in Madison, Indiana; credit Kevin Fleming.

Page 56/57: Used furniture store in Selma, Alabama; credit Flip Schulke.

Page 58/59: Mail box in Chicago, Illinois; reproduced by permission of Travel Ink/Pauline Thorton.

Page 60/61: M & M Cigar Store in Butte, Montana; credit Dave G. Houser.

Page 62/63: "No Standing" sign in New York City; credit Joseph Sohm.

Page 64/65: Downtown Skagway, Alaska; credit Bob Rowan.

Page 66/67: Produce market store front in Palmyra, Wisconsin; credit Richard Hamilton Smith.

Page 68/69: Arthur, Nebraska; credit Philip Gould.

Page 70/71: Crested Butte, Colorado; credit Marc Muench.

Page 72/73: Bannack, Montana; credit Macduff Everton.

Page 74/75: Row of drive-up mail boxes in Lynnwood, Washington; credit Philip James Corwin.

Page 76/77: San Francisco, California; credit Henry Diltz.

Page 78/79: The Shoe Shine man in New York City; credit Roger Wood.

Page 80/81: Fire hydrant in Moab, Utah; credit Henry Diltz.

Page 82/83: Store in Eagles Mere, Pennsylvania; credit Bob Krist.

Page 84/85: Mural in Superior, Nebraska; credit Kevin Fleming.

Page 86/87: General Store in Old Tucson, Arizona; credit Charles and Josette Lenars.

Page 88/89: Manchester, Vermont; credit Paul Thompson.

Page 90/91: Signs in New York City; reproduced by permission of Travel Ink/Andrew Cowin.

Page 92/93: Traffic light in Woodinville, Washington; credit Philip James Corwin.

Page 94/95: Store fronts in Telluride; credit Joseph Sohm.

Page 96/97: St. Croix General Store, Minnesota; credit Richard Hamilton Smith.

Page 98/99: Hutchinson, Kansas; credit Philip Gould.

Page 100/101: Road sign; credit Joseph Sohm.

Page 102/103: Fire Department in Nevada City, Montana; credit Carol Cohen.

Page 104/105: Hurricane, Utah; credit Dewitt Jones.

Page 106/107: Saloon in Nevada city, California; credit Craig Lovell.

Attributions

Page 10/11: Theodore Roosevelt.

Page 14/15: Anon.

Page 16/17: George Burns.

Page 20/21: Anon.

Page 22/23: Ralph Waldon Emerson.

Page 24/25: Anon.

Page 26/27: Popular saying.

Page 30/31: Anon.

Page 32/33: Ralph Waldon Emerson.

Page 34/35: Anon.

Page 38/39: Ronald Reagan.

Page 42/43: Mark Twain.

Page 46/47: Mark Twain.

Page 48/49: Zelda Fitzgerald.

Page 50/51: Anon.

Page 54/55: American proverb.

Page 56/57: Anon.

Page 58/59: Anon.

Page 60/61: Anon.

Page 62/63: Anon.

Page 64/65: Ronald Blythe.

Page 66/67: Rosalind Russell.

Page 68/69: Anon.

Page 70/71: Anon.

Page 72/73: Daniel Boone.

Page 74/75: Anon.

Page 80/81: Steven Wright.

Page 82/83: Anon.

Page 84/85: Anon.

Page 88/89: Mark Twain.

Page 90/91: Anon.

Page 92/93: Anon.

Page 96/97: Carrie Fisher.

Page 98/99: Anon.

Page 102/102: Albert Einstein.

Page 106/107: Popular misquote of Mae West's "Why don't you come up sometime and see me?"

Designer: WDA
Editor: Alison Moss
Researcher: Suzie Green

Sourcebooks, Inc.
P.O. Box 4410, Naperville, Illinois 60567-4410
(630) 961-3900
FAX: (630) 961-2168

Printed and bound in Spain by Bookprint, S.L, Barcelona

MQ 10 9 8 7 6 5 4 3 2 1

ISBN: 1-57071-594-7